ELLIOTT CARTER

TRE DUETTI

for violin and violoncello

HENDON MUSIC

BOOSEY & HAWKES

AN IMAGEM COMPANY

DISTRIBUTED BY

HAL•LEONARD®
CORPORATION

7777 W. BLUEMOUND RD. P.O. BOX 13819 MILWAUKEE, WI 53213

www.boosey.com
www.halleonard.com

Published by Hendon Music, Inc.,
a Boosey & Hawkes company
229 West 28st Street, 11th Fl
New York NY 10001

www.boosey.com

 AN IMAGEM COMPANY

ISMN: 979-0-051-10680-6

First performed on February 11, 2010
at Paul Hall, The Julliard School, New York, NY
by Rolf Schulte; violin and Fred Sherry; violoncello

COMPOSER'S NOTE

Tre Duetti for violin and cello contains the two duets, *Duettone* and *Duettino*, and adds an *Adagio*, which separates the two. Both *Duettone* and *Duettino* were previously published and given their first performance, as well as recorded, by Rolf Schulte and Fred Sherry. These are dedicated to my good friend Milton Babbitt and were written for those wonderful instrumentalists Rolf Schulte and Fred Sherry, who had asked me many times to write for their instruments.

–Elliott Carter

ANMERKUNG DES KOMPONISTEN

Tre Duetti für Violine und Violoncello enthält die beiden *Duette*, *Duettone* und *Duettino* und ebenso ein Adagio, das die beiden trennt. Sowohl *Duettone* und *Duettino* wurden zuvor veröffentlicht. Die Uraufführung spielten und nahmen Rolf Schulte und Fred Sherry auf. Ich widme *True Duetti* an meinen guten Freund Milton Babbitt. Sie wurden für die wunderbaren Instrumentalisten Rolf Schulte und Fred Sherry, welche mich oft fragten für ihre Instrumente zu schreiben, geschrieben.

–Elliott Carter

NOTE DU COMPOSITEUR

Tre Duetti pour violon et violoncelle contient deux duos, *Duettone* et *Duettino*, et ajoute un *Adagio* qui sépare les deux. *Duettone* et *Duettino* ont déjà été publiés et créés ainsi qu'enregistrés par Rolf Schulte et Fred Sherry. Ils sont dédiés à mon cher ami Milton Babbitt et ont été écrits pour les instrumentistes merveilleux Rolf Schulte et Fred Sherry qui m'ont demandé à plusieurs reprises d'écrire pour leurs instruments.

–Elliott Carter

to Milton Babbitt

TRE DUETTI

for Rolf and Fred

DUETTONE

Elliott Carter
(2009)

979-0-051-10680-6

CARTER: *Duettone*

CARTER: *Duettone*

CARTER: *Duettone*

CARTER: *Duettone*

6

NYC
Jan. 21, 2009

CARTER: *Duettone*

ADAGIO

Elliott Carter
(2009)

9

NYC
Dec. 22, 2009

CARTER: *Adagio*

DUETTINO

Elliott Carter
(2008)

CARTER: *Duettino*

CARTER: *Duettino*

CARTER: *Duettino*

14

CARTER: *Duettino*

NYC
May 11, 2008